Talking to Brick Walls

A Series of Presentations
in the Chapel at
Sainte-Anne Hospital

Jacques Lacan

Translated by A. R. Price

polity

First published in French as *Je parle aux murs.*
Entretiens de la chapelle de Sainte-Anne, © Éditions du Seuil, 2011

This English edition © Polity Press, 2017

Polity Press
65 Bridge Street
Cambridge CB2 1UR, UK

Polity Press
101 Station Landing
Suite 300,
Medford, MA 02155, USA

ISBN-13: 978-0-7456-8242-6

A catalogue record for this book is available from the British Library.

Typeset in 12.5 on 15 pt Adobe Garamond by
Servis Filmsetting Ltd, Stockport, Cheshire
Printed and bound by Clays Ltd, St Ives PLC

The publisher has used its best endeavours to ensure that the URLs for external
websites referred to in this book are correct and active at the time of going to
press. However, the publisher has no responsibility for the websites and can
make no guarantee that a site will remain live or that the content is or will
remain appropriate.

Every effort has been made to trace all copyright holders, but if any have been
inadvertently overlooked the publisher will be pleased to include any necessary
credits in any subsequent reprint or edition.

For further information on Polity, visit our website: politybooks.com

Talking to Brick Walls

Contents

v

Note on the Text

Having been invited to deliver a series of monthly seminars for junior psychiatrists at the Sainte-Anne Hospital in Paris, Lacan chose the title *The Psychoanalyst's Knowledge*. Some of his pupils, perhaps inspired by reading Bataille, had at the time been waving the banner of 'non-knowledge'.

While the first three of these *entretiens*, as Lacan called them, corresponded roughly to his initial idea, the next four revolved around questions that were being discussed in his main Seminar held in the Law Faculty on the place du Panthéon under the title ... *or Worse*.

I have respected this caesura by inserting these four sessions in their chronological position in Book XIX of the Seminar, where they would have been a conspicuous omission had they not been included. The first three talks, on the other hand, would be distracting there, and so I have grouped them together in this short book.

They were delivered in the hospital chapel on 4 November 1971, 2 December of the same year, and 6 January 1972.

Jacques-Alain Miller

I
Knowledge, Ignorance, Truth and Jouissance

Coming back to speak at Sainte-Anne I should have hoped there might be some junior doctors here. In my time they were known as asylum interns. Nowadays they work in psychiatric hospitals, not to mention the rest.

They were the audience I had in mind by coming back here to Sainte-Anne. I was hoping that some of them might put themselves out. If any of them are here – I mean doctors who are currently interns – would they be kind enough to raise a hand? That's a crushing minority, but well, it'll do me fine.

On this basis, and so long as I don't run out of steam, I'm going to try to say a few words.

As always, these words are extemporary, which doesn't mean I don't have a few brief notes here. I extemporized them this morning, because I work a great deal. You shouldn't think you have to do as much.

I have insisted on the distance that lies between work and knowledge. Don't forget that this evening I'm promising you some knowledge, so there's no real need to tire yourselves out. You're going to see why. A few of you already have some inkling, having been present at what is known as my Seminar.

To turn to this knowledge, I said at a time that is already long past that in Buddhism, ignorance may be considered a passion. This is a fact that can be accounted for with a little meditation. However, since meditation is not our forte, the only way to become acquainted with it is through experience.

This was an experience that left its mark on me a long while ago, over in the on-call room, because I used to spend time between these walls, a good while back, though not especially these walls here. It was round about 1925–6. At that time, and I'm not speaking about how they are now, as far as ignorance is concerned, the interns were over their heads in it. It was doubtless a group effect. We may consider this to have been a particular period in medicine. It was inevitable that it would be succeeded by the present vacillation.

I've just said that ignorance is a passion. In my opinion, this does not make it of lesser worth, nor is it a deficiency. It's something else. Ignorance is linked to knowledge. It's a way of establishing knowledge, of turning it into established knowledge. For example, back at that time, which of course was the end of an era, when you wanted to be a doctor, well, it was normal for you to display an ignorance that was, so to speak, consolidated.

After what I've just told you about ignorance, it will come as no surprise if I say that a certain cardinal, at a time when this title was not a certificate of ignorance, gave the term *docta ignorantia* to the highest form of knowledge. To remind you in passing, his name was Nicolaus Cusanus. We need to start from this correlation between ignorance and knowledge.

If, at a certain point, in a certain region, ignorance brings knowledge down to its lowest level, this is not the fault of ignorance. It's even the opposite.

For some time now, ignorance in medicine has not been sufficiently learnèd for the latter to survive on anything other than superstition. I will come back to the meaning of this word later, if I have the time, and specifically concerning medicine. But to point out a fact that comes from the experience I'm seeking to get back in touch with, after forty-five years of frequenting these walls – this is not boasting, but ever since I had a few of my writings poubellished,[1] everyone has known how old I am, it's one of the drawbacks of the thing – I must say that the degree of passionate ignorance that reigned back then in the on-call room at Sainte-Anne was, let's say, unmentionable.

It's true that they were the people who had a vocation for it, and at the time to have a vocation for asylums was something fairly peculiar.

In that same on-call room, four people rolled up at the same time, whose names I cannot be averse to uttering again, for I was one of them. The other whom it will please me to conjure up this evening was Henri Ey.

It may be said, with the time that has elapsed since then, that Ey was the civilizer of this ignorance. I commend his work. As Freud noted, civilization doesn't remove discontent, quite the contrary. But in the end, *das Unbehagen*, being *ill at ease*, has a precious side to it.

If you believe that there is the faintest degree of irony in what I've just told you, you are sorely mistaken, but you cannot help but be mistaken because you cannot imagine the level of ignorance in the asylum setting before Ey got involved. It was something quite spectacular.

History has since moved on, and I've just received a memo conveying the alarm that is being felt in one region of this setting with regard to a movement that is promising to set sparks flying, by the name of antipsychiatry. People want a position to be taken on this.

Can one take a position on something that is already an opposition? Undoubtedly it would be a good thing for me to make a few remarks about this, inspired by my long experience, the experience I've just been speaking about, to discriminate on this occasion between psychiatry and *psychiatrizing*.

The question of the mentally ill or, to put it better, of the psychoses, is not resolved in the least by antipsychiatry, regardless of the illusions that some local initiatives maintain on this score. The sense of the antipsychiatry movement is liberation from the psychiatrist, if I dare say so. And this is certainly a long way off.

It's a long way off because there is one characteristic that shouldn't be forgotten in what are called revolutions, which is that the word has been admirably selected to mean *return to the starting point*. The cycle of all this was already familiar, but has been amply demonstrated in Michel Foucault's book, *History of Madness*. Psychiatrists effectively perform a social service. They are the product of a particular historical turning point. The turning point that we are living through is not about to lighten this load, nor to scale down the place it occupies. This is the least one can say about it, which leaves the questions of antipsychiatry in a somewhat awkward situation.

This is an introductory intimation, but I would like to point out that as far as the on-call rooms are concerned there is, even so, something quite striking, and which to my mind forms a continuity between the old and the most recent, and this is the extent to which psychoanalysis has improved nothing with regard to the channels taken by different forms of knowledge.

The psychoanalyst – I raised this question in the academic year of 1967–8, when I introduced the notion of *the psychoanalyst*, preceded by a definite article, a definite article the logical value of which I was trying to inculcate in a fairly large audience – the psychoanalyst doesn't seem to have changed anything with regard to a particular seat of knowledge.

There's nothing irregular about this. Changing the seat of knowledge is not the kind of thing that just happens overnight. The future belongs to God, as they say, that is, to good luck, the good luck of those who had the bright idea of following me. Something will come of them, so long as the bogeyman doesn't get them. This is what I call good luck. For the rest, good luck is out of the question. Their doings will be settled by automatism, which is the exact opposite of luck, good or hard.

For the latter, those whom I'm dooming to what they reckon they're good for, inasmuch as the psychoanalysis they employ doesn't leave them any luck, I would like this evening to avoid a misunderstanding that could arise in the name of something that is a repercussion of the good-will of some followers of mine.

They heard fairly well, as well as they can, what I said about knowledge as a fact of this correlate of ignorance, and this troubled them somewhat. I don't know what got into some of them, it was something literary of course, stuff lying around in the writings of Georges Bataille, for instance, because otherwise I don't think they would have come across it. I'm referring to non-knowledge.

George Bataille gave a lecture on non-knowledge. This non-knowledge is perhaps lying around in two or three spots in his writings. Well, goodness knows he didn't have a field day with it. In particular, on the day of his lecture in the Salle de géographie in Saint-Germain-des-Près, which you are familiar with because it's a place of culture, he didn't utter a single word, which was not a bad way of making a display of non-knowledge.

People jeered, and they were wrong to, because non-knowledge is all the rage nowadays. You can find it all over the place in the mystics. It even emanates from them. It's even with them that it means something. And then, we know that I've insisted on the difference between knowledge and truth. So, if truth is not knowledge, then it's non-knowledge. That's Aristotelian logic – all that is not black is non-black. Since I remarked that the analytic discourse lies precisely on the palpable frontier between truth and knowledge, well, there you go, the path was cleared for the banner of non-knowledge to be raised. It's not such a bad banner. It can serve to rally what it is not excessively uncommon to recruit by way of clientele, crass ignorance, for example. That exists too, though it's increasingly uncommon.

However, there are other things, other aspects, like sloth, for example, which I've been speaking about for a long while. And then there are certain types of institutionalization – the good Lord's concentration camps, as people used to say[2] – within the university system, where these things are welcome, because they're all the rage. In short, one gives oneself over to a whole lot of mimicry. You go first, Lady Truth, the *trou*, the hole, is just down there, and that's your place.

In the end, this non-knowledge is a *trou-vaille*, a find. There's no better when it comes to introducing lasting confusion on a delicate subject, the point in question in psychoanalysis, which I've just called the palpable frontier between truth and knowledge.

Ten years previously, another find was made, which wasn't bad either, in relation to what I really do have to call my discourse. I started by saying that *the unconscious was structured like a language*. A wonderful thing was found – the two fellows who were best suited for spinning that thread were given quite a nice piece job to do, a *Vocabulary of Philosophy*. What am I saying? A *Vocabulary of Psychoanalysis*.[3] Did you catch my slip of the tongue? Well, it's on a par with the *Lalande*.

Someone in the audience – Lalangue?

No, not ... *gue*, it's ... *de*. *Lalingua*, as I write it now, in one word, is something else. You see how cultivated they are!

I didn't say that the unconscious is structured like lalingua, but like a language, and I'll be coming back to this later. But when the respondents whom I just mentioned were set the task of establishing a vocabulary of psychoanalysis, it was clearly because I had put this Saussurian term, *la langue*, on the agenda, which, I repeat, I now write in one word, and I'll be giving the justification for this. Well, lalingua has nothing to do with the dictionary, whatever kind of dictionary it is.

The dictionary has to do with diction, that is to say, with poetry, for instance, with rhetoric. That's no small matter, is it? It extends from invention to persuasion. This is very important, but it's precisely not this dimension that has to do with the unconscious. Contrary to what the masses of candidates think, the unconscious has first and foremost to do with grammar. Even so, a fair share of them do already know this, if they have heeded the few terms by which I've tried to clear a path for what I've been saying about the unconscious. This also has a bit to do, or much to do, or everything to do, with *repetition*, that is, with the aspect that is entirely the opposite of what a dictionary is used for. Therefore, getting them – the very pair who back then could have helped me blaze my trail – to put together a dictionary was a fairly sure way of making them drift away. Grammar and repetition constitute a completely different aspect from what I've just pinpointed as invention, which is doubtless no small matter, and nor is persuasion.

Contrary to what is still very widespread, and I don't know why, the useful aspect in the function of *la langue* – useful for us psychoanalysts, for those who deal with the unconscious – is logic.

This is a brief aside that joins up with the fact that, in the absolutely improvised and mythical promotion that is being propelled by this non-knowledge, there is a risk of losing something. Really, I have offered no occasion for any mistake to be made about this. Is there any need to demonstrate that, in psychoanalysis, there is such a thing as fundamental and primary knowledge? Nevertheless, this is what I'm going to have to demonstrate to you.

Let's hook this primary and solid character of the primacy of knowledge in psychoanalysis by one end.

Do you need reminding that when Freud was trying to account for the difficulties of clearing the path of psychoanalysis, he published an article in *Imago*, in 1917 if I remember rightly, which was translated and published in the first issue of the *International Journal of Psychoanalysis* under the title *A Difficulty in the Path of Psychoanalysis*? It's about the fact that the knowledge involved does not come across easily. Freud explains it as best he can, and this is even how he courts misunderstanding.

It's no accident. I believe I've managed, at least in one particular region, to get them to stop harping on about the famous term *resistance*. But it's quite certain that there is another region where the term still flourishes. For Freud, resistance is clearly a constant apprehension. I daresay we all have our slippages, and they are fostered above all else by resistances. Given time, some will be uncovered in what I have said ... well, that's not entirely sure.

Anyhow, Freud falls wide of the mark. He thinks there is only one thing to be done to overcome resistance, and that is revolution. And so he masks over entirely what is at issue, namely the very specific difficulty that there is in making a certain function of knowledge come into play. He confuses this with what he pinpoints as a revolution in knowledge.

It is in this short article – he will take this up again later in *Civilization and Its Discontents* – that there is the first big chunk on the Copernican Revolution. This was a commonplace in academic knowledge at the time. Copernicus – poor Copernicus! – brought about a revolution. He was the one – so they say in the textbooks – who put the Sun at the centre and made the Earth turn around it. It is utterly clear that, in spite of the diagram in *De revolutionibus* that does indeed show this, Copernicus took no stand whatsoever on that score, and no one dreamed of trying to pick a quarrel with him about it. But in the end, it's a fact that we did indeed go from geo- to heliocentrism, and that this was supposed to have struck a *blow*, as the English text has it, to goodness knows what cosmological narcissism.

Freud evokes a second blow for us, a *biological blow* at the time of Darwin, on the pretext that, as with the Earth, it took people a while to come to terms with the news. This time the new headline made man a close cousin of the euprimates. And then Freud explains the resistance to psychoanalysis as follows – what has been dealt a blow is, strictly speaking, the consistency of knowledge that means that when one knows something, the least one can say about it is that one knows that one knows it. That's the core of it.

Some heavy daubing shapes an ego around that. Namely, the one who knows that he knows is the ego. It's clear that this reference to the ego is secondary in relation to the fact that a knowledge is known, and that the novelty that psychoanalysis reveals is that this is a knowledge that is unknown to itself. But I ask you, what is new in all that, or even likely to give rise to resistance, if this knowledge was in the very nature of a whole world, an animal world, where no one dreams of marvelling at how an animal knows, by and large, what it needs? If it's an earthbound animal, it doesn't go immersing itself in water beyond a limited time. It knows that this holds no value for it. If the unconscious is something surprising it's because this kind of knowledge is something else. We've always had some idea of this knowledge, but how poorly founded this idea was, since people have evoked inspiration, enthusiasm and so on. The unknown knowledge at issue in psychoanalysis is a knowledge that is well and truly articulated, that is structured like a language.

Thus, it transpires that the revolution that Freud pushes to the fore tends to mask over what is at issue. What doesn't come across, revolution or not, is a subversion that is produced in the function, in the structure, of knowledge.

In truth, setting aside the upset that this caused for a few doctors of theology, one cannot really say that the cosmological revolution was likely to make mankind feel humbled in any way. Freud's use of the term *revolution* is scarcely convincing because the very fact that there was a revolution in this regard is rather uplifting as far as narcissism is concerned.

The same goes for Darwinism. There is no other doctrine that puts human production at a higher level than evolutionism.

In both cases, cosmological or biological, each of these revolutions still leaves man in his place as the cream of creation.

This is why Freud's reference truly is poorly inspired. Perhaps it was designed precisely to mask over and bring across what is at issue, namely that this new status of knowledge must entail a new type of discourse, one that is not easy to maintain and which, up to a certain point, has yet to be begun.

I said the unconscious is structured like a language. Which language? And why did I say *a language*?

We're starting to know a thing or two about language. They speak about object-language in logic, whether mathematical or otherwise. They speak of metalanguage. They've even been speaking for a while now about language at the level of biology. They speak about language undiscerningly.

To begin with, I shall say that if I speak about language it's because it's a matter of common features to be met in speech. Though this speech is subject to very high variety, there are still consistent patterns. As I took the time, the care, the trouble and the patience to spell out, the language at issue is the one in which one may distinguish, amongst other things, between code and message. Without this minimal distinction there is no place for speech. This is why, when I introduce these terms, I give them the title *Function and field of speech* – that's the function, *and language* – that's the field.

Speech defines the place of what is called truth. As soon as it makes its entrance, I emphasize, for the use I want to make of it, its structure of fiction, that is to say, equally its structure of mendacity. In truth – quite literally on this occasion – truth speaks the truth, and not by half, only in one case. When it says, *I'm lying*. This is the only case in which one can be sure truth is not lying, because it is presumed to know it. But Otherwise, that is, *Autrement*, with a capital A, it's quite possible that truth none the less speaks the truth without knowing it. This is what I tried to mark out with my capital S, brackets, capital A, the said A being, precisely, barred – S(Ⱥ). At any rate, for those who follow me, you can't say that this, at least, is not a knowledge, or that it's not to be taken into account as a means of guidance, even if only in the short term. This is the first point regarding the unconscious structured like a language.

To find out the second point, you didn't have to wait for me – I'm speaking to the psychoanalysts – because it's the very principle of what you do whenever you interpret.

There is not a single interpretation that does not concern the link between what is made manifest, in what you hear, through speech, and jouissance. It may be that you do this innocently, without ever having realized that not one interpretation ever means anything else, but in the end an analytic interpretation always works like that. Whether the benefit is secondary or primary, the benefit is one of jouissance.

Freud wrote as much, but not straightaway, because there is a stage, the stage of the pleasure principle. But it's quite clear that what struck him one day was that, whatever you do, innocently or otherwise, what gets formulated is something that repeats.

The instance, I said, *of the letter*. And I didn't use *instance* without good reason, which is the case with each and every use I make of words. *Instance* resonates both at the level of judicature and at the level of insistence, where it brings to the surface the modulus that I defined as an *instant*, at the level of a certain logic.

With repetition, Freud discovered the beyond of the pleasure principle. Yet there you have it, if there is a beyond, then let's not speak any more in terms of principle. A principle where there is a beyond is no longer a principle. By the same stroke, let's put aside the reality principle. All of this needs to be revised. There are not two classes of speaking beings, those who steer themselves in accordance with the pleasure principle and the reality principle, and those who are beyond the pleasure principle. Especially given that, clinically speaking, as they say – this being the operative word – they are very much the same.

The primary process was explained at first through this approximation of a pleasure principle/reality principle bipolarity. This rough outline is untenable, and was designed only to get the listeners of the time to swallow these first utterances. Those listeners were bourgeois listeners – I don't want to overuse this term – in other words, they absolutely didn't have the faintest idea about what the pleasure principle is.

The pleasure principle is a reference from the morality of antiquity. In antique morality, pleasure, which consists precisely in making as little as possible of it, *otium cum dignitate*, is an asceticism. It may be said that this pleasure joins up with the pleasure of pigs, but not remotely in the way that people understand it. In antiquity, the word *swine* did not mean *to be a gluttonous hog*. It meant that something was confined to animal sapience. That was a judgement, a touch, a hint, furnished from the outside by people who didn't know what it was about, namely the ultimate refinement of the master's morality. What can that have to do with the idea that the bourgeois man forms of pleasure or, moreover, the idea he forms of reality?

Either way, from the insistence with which the unconscious delivers us what it formulates, there results the following. If our interpretation only ever has the meaning of remarking upon what the subject finds in it, what does he find in it? Nothing that ought not to be catalogued in the register of jouissance. This is the third point.

Point four. Where does jouissance reside? What does it require? It requires a body. To obtain jouissance, you need a body. Even those who promise eternal Beatitude can only do so by presuming that a body will be translated into it. Glorious or otherwise, the body has to be there. Why so? Because for the body, the dimension of jouissance is the dimension of deathward descent.

Moreover, it's in this respect that the pleasure principle announces how Freud knew perfectly well, from that moment forth, what he was saying. If you read it carefully you can see that the pleasure principle has nothing to do with hedonism, even if hedonism has been handed down to us by the most ancient of traditions. In truth, it's the displeasure principle. To the extent that, spelling it out from one moment to the next, Freud slips off course. *In what does pleasure consist?* he asks. And he replies, *in lowering tension*. Yet, why enjoy, if not because it produces a tension? This tension is the very principle of everything that goes by the name of jouissance.

Precisely in this respect, what does Freud tell us in *Civilization and Its Discontents* when he is on the path of the *Jenseits*, the *beyond* of the pleasure principle, if not that, quite probably, far beyond so-called *social suppression* there must be – so he writes, word for word – an *organic suppression*?

It's a shame that one has to go to so much trouble for things said with so much obviousness, to make us perceive the following. The dimension by which the speaking being is distinct from animals is assuredly that in him there is a wide-open gap where he lost his way, where he is allowed to treat the body, or bodies, whether his own or that of his fellow men, or that of the animals around him, in a way that there emerges, for their benefit or for his own, what is called, strictly speaking, jouissance.

In the lines of thought that I've just emphasized, which range from this sophisticated description of the pleasure principle to the open acknowledgement of what is involved in fundamental jouissance, it is assuredly even stranger to see Freud turning to what he designates as a death instinct. Not that this is wrong, it's just that stated in that way, in so learnèd a fashion, this is precisely what the learnèd people he begat under the name of psychoanalysts absolutely could not swallow.

The international psychoanalytic institution is characterized as a whole by lengthy cogitation, lengthy rumination, on the death instinct, with their interminable mazes, their way of being split, of dividing, of fluctuating between accepting it and not accepting it. *I'm stopping right here, I won't follow him that far*. Rather than employ a term that sounds like it's chosen to afford the illusion that something has been discovered in this field, something that one could say is analogous to what in logic is called a paradox, it's astonishing that, given the field he had already cleared, Freud didn't think he needed to give any indication of jouissance, pure and simple. In the realm of erotology, jouissance is truly within anyone's reach. It's true that at that time the publications of the Marquis de Sade were less widely circulated. This was why I thought I should indicate, somewhere in my *Écrits*, the relationship of Kant with Sade. It was a matter of directing attention to it.

Why did Freud go about it in this way? All the same, I think there is an answer to this. It's not necessarily the case that he knew all he was saying any more than any of us do. However, instead of relaying trifles about the primeval death instinct, coming from without or coming from within, or turning back from the outside to the inside to displace itself, somewhat belatedly, into aggressiveness and affray, one could perhaps have read the following in Freud's death instinct. One could have read something that leads us perhaps to say that, all in all, the sole act, if indeed there is one that would be a complete act, would be, if it could be, suicide.

Understand that I'm speaking of an act that would be complete in the same way that last year I was speaking about a discourse that would not be a discourse of semblance. Just as in the one case there is no such discourse, in the other there is no such act.

This is what Freud tells us. He doesn't put it like this, bluntly and plainly, as we are able to put it now, now that the doctrine has cleared its path a little bit and we know that the only acts are failed ones, and that this is even the sole precondition for a semblance of success. This is precisely why suicide is deserving of demur. It doesn't need to remain at the level of an attempt for it to have failed, utterly failed from the standpoint of jouissance. Perhaps not for the Buddhists, with their cans of petrol, because they're in the know. We know nothing about it because they don't come back to bear witness.

Freud's text is an exceedingly fine one. He doesn't put the *soma* and the *germen* before us just for the sake of it.[4] He picks up the scent. He senses that there is something to be dealt with in depth. Indeed, what stands to be gone into in depth – and this is the fifth point, which I've been setting out this year in my Seminar – is stated thus – *there is no sexual relation*.

Like that, it sounds a bit dotty, a bit *éffloupi*.[5] One would just have to get down to some good fucking to demonstrate to me the contrary. Unfortunately, this is something that demonstrates absolutely nothing of the sort because the notion of relation does not altogether coincide with the metaphorical use that is made of the unqualified word *relation*, as in *they had sexual relations*. One can only speak seriously in terms of relation, not simply when a discourse establishes relation, but when relation is stated. The real is there before we think about it, but relation is far more doubtful. Not only do you have to think it through, but also you have to write it down. If you're not bloody capable of writing it down, there's no relation.

It would perhaps be quite remarkable if it were borne out, long enough for it to start to be clarified a little, that it is impossible to write down what would be involved in sexual relation.

This is an important matter precisely because, through the progress of what is called science, we are in the process of pushing very far a heap of tiny things that are located at the level of the gamete, at the level of the gene, at the level of a certain number of selections, of sortings, which are labelled as you like, meiosis or otherwise, and which do indeed seem to clarify something that occurs at the level of the fact that reproduction, at least in a certain area of life, is sexed. Yet this has absolutely nothing to do with what is involved in sexual relation, inasmuch as it is quite certain that in speaking beings there is a range that is altogether admirable in its spread around this relation, inasmuch as this relation is grounded on jouissance.

Two items have been set out by Freud and by the analytic discourse.

On the one hand, there is the full array of jouissance. Everything that can be done to treat a body, particularly one's own body, in a suitable way partakes to some degree of sexual jouissance. However, sexual jouissance itself, when you want to put your finger on it, if I can express it like that, is no longer sexual in the least. It has been lost.

Second, this is where everything that is built around the term *phallus* comes into play. *Phallus* designates a certain signified, the signified of a certain signifier that perfectly fades away, because when it comes to defining what is involved in man or woman, psychoanalysis shows us that this is impossible. Up to a certain degree, nothing is especially indicative of jouissance having to be directed towards the partner of the opposite sex, if jouissance is considered, even quite briefly, to be what guides the reproductive function.

Let's say that, here, we find ourselves faced with the splintering apart of the notion of sexuality. Without a doubt, sexuality lies at the centre of everything that happens in the unconscious. However, it lies at the centre in so far as it is a lack. In other words, in the stead of anything whatsoever of sexual relation that could be written as such, impasses arise, impasses which are generated by the function of sexual jouissance in so far as it appears as the point of mirage that Freud himself makes a note of somewhere as absolute jouissance. And it's at much closer quarters in that, precisely, this jouissance is not absolute.

Jouissance is in no sense absolute because, first of all, as such it is doomed to these different forms of failure constituted by castration for male jouissance and by division for female jouissance. On the other hand, what jouissance leads to has strictly nothing to do with copulation in so far as the latter is, let's say, the usual manner – this is going to change – by which reproduction occurs in the species of speaking beings.

In other words, there is a thesis – *there is no sexual relation*. I'm speaking about the speaking being. There is an antithesis, which is *the reproduction of life*. This is a well-known theme, and is the current banner of the Catholic Church, for which we should salute its stamina. The Catholic Church asserts that there is a sexual relation, the one that culminates in producing little children. This is an assertion that is quite tenable, but it cannot be demonstrated. No discourse can sustain it, except religious discourse in so far as it defines the strict separation that exists between truth and knowledge. Third, there is no synthesis, unless you label as a synthesis the remark that there is no jouissance but by dying.

These are the points of truth and knowledge, in relation to which it is important to stress what is involved in the psychoanalyst's knowledge, with the proviso that there is not a single psychoanalyst for whom this does not go unheeded. For the synthesis, one can trust in them to support its terms and to see them entirely elsewhere than in the death instinct. *Chassez le naturel*, as they say, *il revient au galop*.[6]

Even so, we need to give its true meaning to this old proverbial formula.

Let's speak about the natural. It is everything that is clad in the livery of knowledge, and Lord knows there is no dearth of it. The university discourse is designed solely for knowledge to function as a livery. The apparel at issue is the idea of nature. It is not about to vanish from the forefront of the stage. Not that I'm trying to replace it with another one. Don't imagine that I'm one of those who pit culture against nature, if only because nature is precisely a fruit of culture. But in the end, we haven't even begun to have the faintest beginning of adhesion to this *knowledge/ truth* relationship, or *truth/knowledge*, as you like, no more than to what we say about medicine, psychiatry and a stack of other problems.

Before long, in four or five years' time, we are going to be swamped by problems of segregation, which will be labelled or excoriated with the term *racism*. All these problems hinge on the control of what happens at the level of the reproduction of life in beings who happen to have, by virtue of the fact that they speak, all sorts of problems of conscience. It is extraordinary that people have not yet realized that problems of conscience are problems of jouissance.

But in the end we're only just beginning to be able to express these problems. It's by no means sure that expressing them will have the least consequence, since we know that interpretation requires, in order to be received, what at the start of the talk I was calling *work*. As for knowledge, this belongs to the realm of jouissance. We absolutely cannot see why it would ever switch beds. If people denounce what they call intellectualization, it's simply because they are accustomed from experience to noticing that it is on no account necessary, nor on any account sufficient, to understand something for anything whatsoever to change.

The question of the psychoanalyst's knowledge is not at all as to whether it is articulated or not. Rather, it's about knowing which place one has to be at in order to sustain it. I'll try to give you a hint of this, though I don't know if I'll manage to give it a transmissible formulation.

The question is to find out what science – to which psychoanalysis may be no more than the attendant, nowadays as in Freud's time – can reach that falls within the remit of the term *real*.

As for the might of the symbolic, it doesn't have to be demonstrated. It is might itself. There is no trace of might in the world prior to the appearance of language. In what he sketches out as a pre-Copernican age, Freud imagines to himself that mankind was as happy as can be at the centre of the universe, of which man thought he was king. This is sheer grandiose illusion. If there was something that mankind had an idea of in the eternal spheres, it was precisely that there lay the last word of knowledge. In the world, it is the ethereal spheres that know something. They know. And it would take some time for that to pass. This is why knowledge has been associated from the start with the idea of power.

The short note to be found on the back of the large pack of my *Écrits* mentions the Enlightenment. Why not admit it? I wrote it myself. Who else but me could have done so? My style has been recognized, and it's not badly written at all! The Enlightenment took a while to be elucidated. At first, they really missed the mark. But then, like hell itself, its road was paved with good intentions. Contrary to all that has been said, the goal of the Enlightenment was to set out a knowledge that would not pay homage to any power. Only, people regret to have to note that those who applied themselves in this function were a little too much in the position of valets in relation to a certain type of master – fairly blithe and thriving masters, I must say – the nobility of the time, for them to have been able to come to anything else but the famous French Revolution, which had the result you know, namely the establishment of a race of masters who were more ferocious than any who had previously been seen at work.

From a certain perspective, which I will not qualify as progressive, what the psychoanalyst would be able to convey is a knowledge that can't do anything about it, the knowledge of powerlessness.

To set you the tone of the trail along which I hope to further my disquisition this year, I'm going to let you be the first to know – so, lick your chops – the title of the Seminar I'm going to be delivering on the same site as last year, by the grace of a few people who've been kind enough to dedicate themselves to preserving it for us.

It's written like this. First of all, there are three dots. Then an *o* and an *r*. At the place of these three dots you can put whatever you like. I offer it to your meditation. This *or* is the one that is called *vel* or *aut* in Latin. Then *worse* is added. And this gives ... *or Worse*.

4 November 1971

34

II
On Incomprehension and Other Themes

What I'm doing with you this evening is clearly not what I had planned to do this year, which was to give the next step of my Seminar. It's going to be an *entretien*, like last time.[1]

Everyone knows – many ignore it – my insistence, to those who solicit my counsel, on preliminary *entretiens* in analysis. Of course, it has an essential function for analysis. There is no possible way in to analysis without these preliminary consultations. But something of this comes close to the relationship between these *entretiens* and what I'm going to be saying to you this year, except that it absolutely cannot be the same given that, since I'm the one who is speaking, I'm the one in the position of analysand.

I could have come at this from a good many other angles, but at the end of the day it's invariably at the last minute that I know what I've chosen to say. Today's *entretien* strikes me as a favourable opportunity in view of a question that was put to me yesterday evening by someone from my School, one of those people who take their position to heart. I was asked, word for word, *Is the failure to comprehend Lacan a symptom?*

To my mind, this question has the advantage of leading me straight to the crux of the matter. It is widely known that I seldom do that. I approach things with a cautious step.

I can easily forgive this person for putting my name – which is explained by the fact that she was standing in front of me – in the place of what would have been more appropriate, namely *my discourse*. You see I'm not ducking out. I call it mine. We shall be seeing in a while whether this *my* deserves to be maintained. No matter. The crucial aspect of this question lay in what it bears on, namely whether the incomprehension at issue, regardless of how you label it, is a symptom.

I don't think so. I don't think it is. First of all because in one sense it cannot be said that my speech, which does none the less bear a particular relationship to my discourse, has absolutely not been understood. More to the point, one can say that the number of you here is proof of that. If my speech were incomprehensible, I don't really see what you would be doing here in such large numbers, especially given how these numbers are made up of people who come back.

At the level of a sampling of comments that make their way to me, it sometimes happens that people who express themselves by these channels do not always understand well, or at least do not have the feeling that they understand. To refer to one of the most recent echoes I received, the person in question, despite this feeling of not quite getting it, still declared that it helped her to find her way in her own ideas, to be clearer in her mind on a number of points. It cannot be said, therefore, at least as far as my speech is concerned, which clearly has to be set apart from discourse, that there is incomprehension, strictly speaking.

I will stress right away that this speech is speech designed for teaching. On this occasion, I set teaching apart from discourse. Since I'm speaking here at Sainte-Anne – and perhaps through what I said last time you have been able to sense what this means to me – I've chosen to take things up at what one might call the elementary level. This is completely arbitrary, but it's a choice.

When I went to the French Philosophical Society to make a presentation on what at the time I was calling *my teaching*, I took the same stand. I spoke as though I were addressing people who were somewhat behind. They are no more behind than you are, but it's rather my idea of philosophy that determined that. And I'm not the only one. One of my very good friends who made a recent presentation at the same Society handed me an article on the foundation of mathematics, and I remarked to him that it was at a far higher level, a dozen times higher, than what he'd said to the Society. He replied that there was no cause for astonishment, given the responses he'd received. Since I received responses of the same sort there, I was reassured that I had spelt out some items, which you can find in my *Écrits*, at the same level.

In certain contexts, therefore, there is a less arbitrary choice than the one I'm upholding here. I'm upholding this choice here in view of elements in living memory that are tied to the fact that, at the end of the day, if at a certain level my discourse is still not being understood, let's say that it's because in an entire zone it was long forbidden, not to *l'entendre*, to understand it, which would have been in the range of many, as experience has borne out, but forbidden to *venir l'entendre*, to *come along to hear it*. This is what is going to allow us to set this incomprehension apart from a number of other types. And, my word, that this prohibition was issued by an analytic institution is surely significant.

What does that mean, *significant*? I did not say *of significance*. There is a big difference between the signifier/signified relation and signification. Signification forms a sign. A sign has nothing to do with a signifier.[2] As I have written in a corner somewhere in the most recent issue of my journal *Scilicet*, whatever one may think, a sign is always the sign of a subject. To what is this sign addressed? This is also written in the same *Scilicet*. I can't expand on it now, but this sign of prohibition certainly came from true *subjects*, in every sense of the word, from subjects who obey, in any case. The fact that it was a sign from an analytic institution is just what it takes to lead us to take the next step.

If the question was put to me in this form, it's in view of the following, that incomprehension in psychoanalysis is considered to be a symptom. This has gained acceptance in psychoanalysis. It is widely accepted. It's even got to the point that it has slipped into common consciousness. When I say that it's widely accepted, I mean it's gone beyond psychoanalysis, beyond the analytic act. In the pattern of common consciousness, it's got to the point that people can be heard saying *Go and get yourself psychoanalyzed* when the person who says it reckons that your conduct, your comments, are a symptom. It's become a banality.

I point out to you, even so, that at this level, from this angle, *symptom* has the sense of *truth value*. It is in this respect that what has slipped into public consciousness is more precise, alas, than the idea many psychoanalysts manage to form of it. Let's say that too few of them know about the equivalence between a symptom and a truth value.

This has an historical guarantor, in that it reveals that the meaning of the word *symptom* was discovered and stated before psychoanalysis came on the scene. As I have emphasized fairly often, this equivalence is the essential step taken by Marxist thought.

To translate the symptom into a truth value we need to experience at first hand what is supposed in terms of knowledge in the analyst by the fact that he really ought to be interpreting knowingly.

To make a brief digression here, I shall indicate that this knowledge is, as it were, presupposed of the analyst. This is what I accentuated with regard to the *subject supposed to know* as grounding the phenomena of transference. I've always emphasized how, for the analysand-subject, this does not entail any certainty that his analyst knows all about it. This is very far from being the case. But it's perfectly compatible with the fact that an analysand may consider the analyst's knowledge to be altogether dubious, which moreover is a fairly frequent occurrence, for altogether objective reasons. All in all, analysts don't always know as much about it as they should, for the simple reason that, often, they don't bloody do very much. That changes absolutely nothing about the fact that knowledge is *presupposed* with respect to the function of the analyst, and that the phenomena of transference hinge on that.

This is the end of the digression. Now for the symptom with its translation as truth value.

The symptom is a truth value, but the reverse is not true. The truth value is not a symptom. It's useful to note it at this point for the reason that truth is not remotely related to anything whose function I claim to be isolable. Its function is relative, and in particular where it takes up its place, in speech. It is not separable from other functions of speech. This is another reason for me to insist that, even when reduced to value, truth is not to be confused on any account with a symptom.

The first phases of my teaching revolved around what a symptom is. Indeed, the analysts were in such a muddle on this score that from their lips it was being said that symptoms are a refusal of truth value. After all, perhaps it is owing to my teaching that this is not being put about so freely. What they were saying bears no relation to the equivalence that runs in one direction, from the symptom to a truth value.

This brings into play the Being of an entity.

I'm putting it like this because it's just between us, and because I said that this is an *entretien*. I'm putting it like this without further formality, without concern for the fact that the terms I'm putting forward are already in common use at the most cutting edge of philosophy.

I say *Being* – because, for as long as philosophy has been going round in circles on a number of points, it seems to be the accepted term – because it's a matter of the *être parlant*. It's on account of *being speaking* – excuse me for this first *being* – that the speaking being comes to Being, well, that he has the sense that he does, because naturally he doesn't come to it, he misses it. But one may say that this dimension of Being, which opens up all of a sudden, held sway for a good while over the system ... of philosophers, at the very least.

It would be wrong to poke fun at this because, though it held sway over the philosophers' system, they held sway over everyone else's system. This is what analysts denounce in what they label as resistance. I fought this, during a phase of my teaching the trace of which is preserved in my *Écrits*, in order to question them on what they knew about what they were doing by bringing in the *Being* of this damned *entity* they talk about, not altogether indiscriminately. Once in a while, they call it *mankind*. However, for as long as I've been among those who have voiced a few reservations about this term, people have been using it less and less. This Being has no special tropism towards truth. Let's not say any more on that score.

So, the symptom is a truth value. This is the function that resulted from introducing, at a particular historical moment that I have dated well enough, the notion of *symptom*.

A symptom is not cured in the same way in Marxist dialectic and in psychoanalysis. In psychoanalysis, it has to do with something that is the translation of its truth value into speech. That this should give rise to what is felt by the analyst to be a Being of refusal on no account allows it to be settled as to whether this feeling deserves to be retained in any way, because equally, in other registers, precisely in the register I mentioned earlier, the symptom has to yield to altogether different procedures.

I'm not according preference to any one of these procedures, and even less so given that I want to enable you to hear that there is another dialectic besides the one that is imputed to history.

Between the questions *Is psychoanalytic incomprehension a symptom?* and *Is the failure to comprehend Lacan a symptom?* I would place a third, *Is mathematical incomprehension a symptom?* There are people, young people even, because this is only of interest among young people, for whom this dimension of mathematical incomprehension exists.

When one turns one's attention to these subjects who display mathematical incomprehension, which is still fairly widespread these days, one has the feeling – I'm using the word *sentiment*, feeling, in exactly the same way as I used it earlier for what the analysts did with resistance – that it stems from something akin to dissatisfaction, to disharmony, to something that is experienced in the handling, precisely, of the truth value.

Subjects who are beset by mathematical incomprehension expect more from truth than the reduction to those values that are called, at least on the first steps of mathematics, deductive values. Articulations that are said to be *demonstrative* strike them as lacking something, precisely at the level of a requirement of truth. The *true or false* bivalence puts them to flight, and, let's say it, this is not without good reason. Up to a certain point, one can say that there is a certain distance between truth and what we may call a cipher.[3]

The cipher is nothing else but a written form, the written form of its value. Regardless of whether the bivalence is expressed, depending on the case, in terms of 0 and 1 or T and F, the result is the same, in view of something that appears to be a requisite for some subjects.

You were able to hear earlier that I wasn't speaking about anything that is, in any sense whatsoever, content. On what grounds would one use such a term? *Content* doesn't mean a thing so long as one cannot say what is at issue. A truth has no content. A truth that is said to be such is either truth or else semblance, this being a distinction that has nothing to do with the opposition between true or false, because if it is semblance, it is a semblance, precisely, of truth.

Mathematical incomprehension comes from the question as to whether, truth or semblance, this might not be all One. Allow me to put it like that. I'm going to be returning to it in more erudite fashion in another setting.

In any case, the logical development of mathematics that has been undertaken will certainly not object on this point. Indeed, Bertrand Russell took care to say, word for word, that mathematics is *the subject in which we never know what we are talking about, nor whether what we are saying is true.* He's pushing it somewhat, but it's a way of saying that all the care he lavished on the rigour of formulation in mathematical deduction is something that is assuredly addressed to something utterly different from truth, but which does possess one facet that, all the same, is not unrelated to it, because were it not for that there would be no need to set it apart so emphatically.

It's quite certain that logic – and this is

dissimilar from what is involved in mathematics – which strives to account for mathematical articulation with regard to truth, is being affirmed in our time in a propositional logic that holds that, when truth has been posited as the value that sets the denotation of a given proposition, this true proposition can only obtain another true proposition.

The least one can say is that this seems strange indeed. To spell it right out, *implication* is defined here as the strange genealogy from which it results that, once the true has been reached, it cannot in any way whatsoever, through anything of what it implies, go back to the false. However slim the chances may be that a false proposition should obtain a true proposition – which, moreover, is fully accepted – since the time that people have been *propositioning* in this alley that we are told is without return, there ought henceforth only to be true propositions.[4]

In truth, this statement can only be upheld, even for an instant, due to the existence of mathematics independently of logic. There is a tangle somewhere. The mathematicians themselves are very far from being at ease on this matter, since everything that effectively stimulated this logical research concerning mathematics in all its aspects set off from the sense that non-contradiction is in no way sufficient to ground truth. This does not mean that non-contradiction is not desirable, or even a requisite, but it is certainly not sufficient.

We shan't make any further headway on this score this evening, because this is just an introductory talk to a way of handling things, which is precisely the path I intend to make you follow this year at my Seminar.

This tangle is likely to lead us to the idea that the symptom of mathematical incomprehension is conditioned, in sum, by truth's love for itself, so to speak.

This is something different from the refusal I was speaking about earlier. It's even the contrary, in that one would have succeeded in conjuring away completely any aspect of pathos. Yet this is not how it happens at the level of one way of expounding on mathematics. Illustrating it as I did with the effort of the so-called logician, it is none the less presented in a manageable and ordinary way, without further logical introduction. It is presented in a straightforward and elementary fashion, such that *proof*, as they say, allows several steps to be conjured away. Phenomena of incomprehension are doubtless being produced in young people on account of a particular emptiness that is felt regarding what is involved in the veracity of what is articulated.

It would be quite wrong to think that mathematics is something that has indeed succeeded in emptying the aspect of pathos from everything that is involved in the relation to truth. There is not only elementary mathematics. We know enough history to be aware of the trouble and pain that the terms and the functions of infinitesimal calculus generated at the time of their excogitation, as did the later regularization, ratification and logification of the same terms and methods, and even the introduction of a number that was raised higher and higher, that was increasingly elaborate, the introduction of what at this level we really have to call *mathemes*.[5] The said mathemes do not entail any retrograde genealogy. They do not entail any potential expounding for which the term *historical* would have to be used.

The mathematics of ancient Greece shows perfectly well those points at which, even when it had the good fortune to get close to what came about much later, when infinitesimal calculus went public, it didn't manage it, it didn't take the step.

While it is easy, based on infinitesimal calculus, or, to put it better, based on its perfect reduction, to ascertain and classify what was involved both in the procedures of demonstration in Greek mathematics and in the impasses that were laid out in advance as perfectly ascertainable after the event, we can see that it is absolutely untrue to speak of a matheme as something that would be detached from the requirement of veracity.

Innumerable debates, debates in spoken word, have punctuated the emergence of new mathemes at each moment of history. I have spoken implicitly of Leibniz and Newton, and I'm also thinking of all those who preceded them with incredible audacity in goodness knows what constituent of encounter or adventure, in whose connection the term *tour de force* or *stroke of luck* is brought up. Isaac Barrow, for example.

This was revived in an era very close to our own with Cantor's forceful entry, where nothing is done to diminish what earlier I called the dimension of pathos, a dimension that for Cantor himself extended into the reaches of madness. Nor do I believe that it is adequate to tell us about the ensuing disappointments in his career, the opposition he met, or even the insults that he received from the dominant academics of his time. We are not accustomed to finding madness being prompted by actual persecutions.

Certainly, everything has been laid out to make us ask ourselves about the function of matheme.

Mathematical incomprehension must, therefore, be something different from a requirement that would arise in some way from a formal emptiness. Judging by what has occurred in the history of mathematics, it's not certain that this incomprehension is not generated by some relation between the matheme, even the most elementary matheme, and a dimension of truth. It is perhaps those who are most sensitive who comprehend the least.

We already have some notion of this at the level of what remains of the Socratic dialogues, of what we may presume of them. After all, there are people for whom, perhaps, the encounter with truth plays the role that the aforesaid Greeks borrowed from a metaphor – it has the same effect as contact with a torpedo ray. It stuns them. This idea stems from the contribution – doubtless a confused contribution, but this is what metaphors are for – that makes a meaning rise up that far outstrips its means. The torpedo ray, and then the person who touches it and goes numb, is plainly an encounter between two fields that have no accord between them, though this wasn't yet known at the time the metaphor was wrought. *Field*, here, is being taken in the proper sense of *magnetic field*.

I would point out to you that everything we have just touched on, and which culminates in the word *field*, is constituted by what the other day I called, via a slip of the tongue, *lalingua*. *Field* is the word I used when I said *Function and field of speech and language*. The field under consideration here, turning incomprehension as such into the key to it, is precisely what allows us to exclude all psychology from it.

The fields at issue are constituted by the real, which is just as real as the torpedo ray and the innocent finger that has just touched it. Just because we make our approach to the matheme along the paths of the symbolic, this doesn't mean that it's not a matter of the real.

The truth in question in psychoanalysis is what, by means of language – I mean through the function of speech – approaches something that is real.

However, this approach is on no account the inroad of cognizance, but rather, I would say, the inroad of something like induction, with the meaning this term possesses in the constitution of a field. It's about the induction of something that is utterly real, although we can only speak about it in terms of signifiers. I mean that they have no other existence but that of signifiers.

What am I speaking about? Well, about nothing other than what in everyday language are known as men and women. We know nothing real about these men and these women as such.

This is what is at stake, not dogs and bitches. What is at stake is what it is *really* about, with respect to those who belong to either sex on the basis of *l'être parlant*.[6] There is not the faintest shadow of psychology here. Men and women, that's real, but in their regard we are incapable of articulating the slightest thing in lalingua that would bear the slightest relation to this real. Psychoanalysis cannot help but harp on about this.

This is what I am stating when I say that there is no sexual relation for beings who speak. Why so? Because their speech, such as it functions, is conditioned as speech by the fact that this sexual relation is very precisely, as speech, prohibited from functioning in any way that might allow one to account for it.

I'm not giving primacy to anything in this correlation. I'm not saying that speech exists because there is no sexual relation. That would be absurd. Nor am I saying that there is no sexual relation because speech is there. But there is certainly no sexual relation because speech functions on a level that happens to have been uncovered, by way of the psychoanalytic discourse, as specifying the speaking being, namely the pre-eminence of everything that will turn sex into semblance, the semblance of blokes and of *bonnes femmes*, as people used to say after the last war. They didn't label them any differently – *bonnes femmes*. This is not quite how I'm going to be speaking about them, because I'm no existentialist.

Either way, that this should be constituted through the fact that the *entity* speaks, the fact that this essential point is derived only from speech, is on this occasion to be distinguished entirely from sexual relation. This essential point is jouissance, the jouissance that is called sexual, and which determines, in this entity I've been speaking about, the very thing it is a matter of obtaining, namely coupling. Psychoanalysis makes us face up to the fact that everything depends on this pivotal point that is called sexual jouissance.

However, it turns out that sexual jouissance may be articulated in a coupling of duration, or even one that is momentary, solely if it involves an encounter with castration, which possesses no dimension except in lalingua. The only thing that allows us to affirm this are the comments we garner in the psychoanalytic experience.

The articulation of this opaque kernel called sexual jouissance strikes me as being altogether deserving of an effort to formulate the matheme for it. I point out to you that the articulation to be explored in this register, which is called castration, dates merely from the historically recent emergence of the psychoanalytic discourse. The effort in question is for something to be demonstrated, differently from what is merely endured, endured in a kind of shameful secret which, on account of having been made public by psychoanalysis, remains none the less shameful and bereft of outcome. No one seems to have noticed that the question lies at the level of the entire dimension of jouissance, namely, the speaking being's relation to his body, for there is no other possible definition of jouissance.

What animal species derives jouissance from its body, and how? We certainly have traces of this in our cousins the chimpanzees, who delouse each other with all the signs of keenest attention. Why is it that in speaking beings this relationship to jouissance is far more elaborate? Psychoanalysis discovered that this is due to the fact that sexual jouissance emerges earlier than the maturity that is qualified with the same adjective. This seems to suffice to render *infantile* the array of different types of jouissance that are qualified as perverse, which is no doubt a limited array, but not lacking in variety.

This is closely related to the enigma that means that we cannot do anything with what seems to be directly linked to the operation that sexual jouissance is presumed to target, and which also means that we can on no account head this way, where the pathways abide by speech, without it being articulated in castration. It's curious that this was never noticed. I don't want to speak in terms of an *attempt* because, as Picasso said, *I don't seek, I find*, that is, *I don't attempt, I make a decisive slice*, but this was never noticed prior to my making the decisive slice to show that the key point, the nodal point, is lalingua, and within the field of lalingua, the operation of speech.

There is not one analytic interpretation that is not designed to isolate, in whatever proposition one may meet, its relationship to a jouissance. What does psychoanalysis say? It says that, in this relationship with jouissance, it is speech that assures its dimension of truth. And, still, it remains no less assured that speech cannot tell the truth completely. It can only, as I have expressed it, *half-say* this relationship, and forge a semblance thereof, the semblance of what is called a man or a woman.

One makes something of it, without being able to say much about it. One cannot say a great deal about the type.

A couple of years ago I managed to articulate, on the trail I've been trying to blaze, what is involved in four discourses.

These discourses are not historical discourses. It's not mythology, and it's not Rousseau's nostalgia, nor even Neolithic nostalgia, these being things that only concern the university discourse. The university discourse never fares better than at the level of bodies of knowledge that no longer mean anything to anyone, because the university discourse is constituted by turning knowledge into semblance.

These four discourses constitute, in a palpable way, something of the real. We live within this borderline relationship between the symbolic and the real. Make no mistake.

The discourse of the master is still holding fast. It goes on and on. I think you have enough first-hand experience of this for me not to have to indicate what I could have indicated if it had amused me, that is, if I were striving to be more popular. I could have shown you the little twist that turns it into the discourse of the capitalist. It's exactly the same gismo, only it's better made. It functions better. It leaves you even further up the creek. Either way, you don't even think about it. It's the same as with the university discourse. You're up to your ears in it, when you think you're having a riot, the *émoi de mai*.[7]

Don't even mention the hysteric discourse, which is the scientific discourse itself. It's very important to be acquainted with this, so as to make some little prognoses. It diminishes nothing of the merits of scientific discourse.

If one thing is certain it's that I was only able to articulate these three discourses in a sort of matheme because the analytic discourse came about. And when I speak of the analytic discourse, I'm not speaking about something that belongs to the realm of cognizance. For a long time now it's been possible to notice that the discourse of cognizance is a sexual metaphor, and to learn the lesson from that, namely that since there is no sexual relation, there is no cognizance either. For centuries we lived with a sexual mythology, and of course a large share of analysts ask for nothing more than to revel in these cherished memories of an inconsistent era. But this is not what's at stake. As I have written on the first line of something I'm currently cogitating, so as to deliver it to you in a short while – *that which is said is de facto, by the fact of saying it.*

Yet there lies the stumbling block. Everything lies there, and everything arises from this. This is what I have called *l'Hachose*. I've put an aitch at the front so that you can see that there is an apostrophe, but I ought not to put one. It should be called *l'Achose*.[8] In short, the object *a*.

The object *a* is certainly an object, but only in the sense that it definitively supersedes any notion of the object as supported by a subject. This is not the relation of cognizance. It's rather curious, when one studies it in detail, to see that in this relation of cognizance, they ended up making it so that one of the terms, the subject in question, was nothing more than the shadow of a shade, a reflection that had perfectly faded away. The object a is an object only in the sense that it is there to affirm how nothing in the realm of knowledge can fail to produce it. This is something utterly different from taking cognizance of it.

The psychoanalytic discourse can only be articulated by showing that, in order for there to be some chance of an analyst, a certain operation which is called the psychoanalytic experience needs to have carried the object a to the place of semblance. It would be absolutely unable to occupy this place were the other elements, which are reducible in a signifying chain, not occupying the other places. If the subject, along with what I call the master signifier and what I designate as the corpus of knowledge, were not shared out across the four points of a tetrahedron – which, so that you can take it easy, I've drawn on the blackboard in the shape of vectors that cross within a square that is open on one side – it's clear that there would be no discourse.

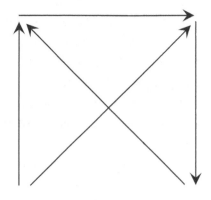

I say that what defines discourse, and contrasts it with speech, is that it is determined, for the speaking approach, by the real. This is what a matheme is. The real I'm speaking about is absolutely inapproachable except along a mathematical path. To ascertain this, there is no other path but this discourse, the last of the four to come on the scene, the one I define as the analytic discourse. In a way that it would be inordinate to call consistent, because on the contrary it harbours a wide-open gap, and specifically the gap that is expressed by the thematic of castration, the analytic discourse enables us to see where the real that this entire discourse hinges on is assured.

In conformity with everything that is accepted in analysis, the real I speak about is that nothing is assured regarding what seems to be the finality of sexual jouissance, of copulation, without these steps that are glimpsed altogether confusedly, but which are never isolated in a structure comparable to the structure of a logic, and which is called castration.

It is very precisely in this respect that the effort of logic has to be a model for us, even a guide. And don't press me to speak about isomorphism. The fact that there is a fearless little rascal from academia who reckons my statements on truth, semblance, jouissance and surplus jouissance are formalist, even hermeneutic ... why not? It's rather a matter of what in mathematics is known as a *generator* operation. It's a curious thing, and it's an encounter. This year, at a different location from this one here, we are going to try prudently to approach what is at issue, from afar, and step by step. One shouldn't expect too much from the sparks that might fly, but it will come in due course.

The object *a* I spoke to you about earlier is not

an object. It is what allows each of these four discourses to be made into a tetrahedron in its own
way. Strangely enough, what the analysts can't
see is that the object *a* is not a point that is local-
ized somewhere in the four others or the four that
they form together. It is the construction, it is the
tetrahedral matheme, of these discourses.

The question, therefore, concerns where each
achosique being, each embodied *a* that every one
of us is in some capacity, is most beset by incomprehension of my discourse. The question may
be asked. Whether or not this incomprehension
is a symptom is secondary. But what is altogether
certain is that, theoretically speaking, it's at the
level of the psychoanalyst that incomprehension
of my discourse must dominate, and precisely
because it is the analytic discourse.

Perhaps it's not the privilege of the analytic
discourse. After all, the one who pushed furthest
the discourse of the master, before I brought my
object *a* into the world, and who clearly made
a mess of it because he wasn't acquainted with
the object *a*, was Hegel, to cite him by name.
He always said that if there was one person
who understood nothing of the discourse of the
master, then it was the master himself. Hegel

thereby remains rooted in psychology, because there is no master. There is a master signifier, and the master follows as best he can. This does not facilitate in the least the master's understanding of the master discourse. It is in this sense that Hegel's psychology is accurate.

It would likewise be very hard to maintain that a hysteric, at the point at which she is positioned, namely at the level of semblance, is best placed to understand her discourse. But for that, there would be no need of the turn to analysis. Let's not mention, of course, the university academics. No one has ever quite believed that they have the front to sustain a distraction as tremendously patent as the whole of the university discourse is.

So, why would analysts have the privilege of access to what makes for the matheme of their discourse? On the contrary, there is every reason for them to set themselves up in a sort of status the interest of which could be to show what ensues from this in those inconceivable theoretical flights of fancy that fill up the journals of the psychoanalytic world. This is not what's important. The important thing is to take an interest, and I shall surely be trying to tell you what this interest can consist of. It needs absolutely to be exhausted in all its facets.

I've just indicated what might be involved in the status of the analyst at the level of semblance. It is no less important to articulate it in its relationship with truth. And what is most interesting – this really is the term because it's one of the only meanings you can give to the word *interest* – is the relation that this discourse has with jouissance, the jouissance that sustains, conditions and accounts for this discourse.

I don't want to end by giving you the idea that I know what mankind is. There are surely people out there who need me to toss them this little fish. After all, I can toss them this fish because it doesn't connote any kind of promise of progress, ... *or worse.* I can tell them that, very probably, what specifies this animal species is an altogether anomalous and strange relationship with jouissance.

This may well have a few minor extensions on the side of biology. Why not? But I observe simply that analysts have not led to the slightest progress being made in the biologizing reference to analysis.

On the other hand, on the side of the biologists, something incredible has been done in the name of this lame and amputated jouissance, castration itself, which in mankind looks like it bears a certain relation to copulation, to that which culminates, biologically, in the conjunction of the sexes, but without it conditioning of course absolutely anything in semblance. There were some biologists who extended this anomalous point, this perfectly problematic relation, to animal species, and they extended perversion to them as well. A large book was put together on the theme, which immediately received the favourable backing of my dear colleague Henri Ey, whom I mentioned last time with a sympathy you were able to note.

In the name of what would there be perversion in animal species? Animals couple, but what proves to us that this is in the name of a jouissance, perverse or otherwise? You really have to belong to mankind to believe that copulating gives rise to jouissance. There are whole tomes on this subject to explain how there are some who do it with hooks, with their little leggies, and then there are some who shoot the sperm straight into the central *bursa*, as is the case for bedbugs, I believe. And then people marvel at the jouissance they must derive from such doings. If we did that with a syringe through the peritoneum, O how voluptuous that would be! People think they can construct accurate things with that, when in fact the first thing to put your finger on is the dissociation of sexual jouissance.

It's quite clear that the only question, the very *interesting* question, is how lalingua, which for the moment we can say is correlative to the disjunction of sexual jouissance, bears an evident relation to something of the real. But how are we to go from here to mathemes that enable us to build science? That truly is the question, the only question. And what if we were to look a little more closely at how science is put together?

I tried to do that for just one brief moment, a tiny little inroad, in my text that carries the title *Science and Truth*.

There was one schmuck, who was hosting me at the time, who fell sick after hearing what I said in that regard. After all, it's precisely here that one can see that my discourse has been understood. He's the only one to have been sickened by it. He was a man who demonstrated in umpteen different ways that he wasn't a particularly hardy fellow, and I have no passion whatsoever for the feeble-minded. In this respect, I'm quite different from my dear friend Maud Mannoni. However, since one also meets feeble-minded folk at the Institute, I don't see why I should get upset.

Anyhow, *Science and Truth* was an attempt to broach a little something along those lines. This notorious science may well be made up of practically nothing, in which case one would be better able to explain how appearance, which is conditioned by a deficit just as much as lalingua, can lead straight to it.

There you go. These are questions that perhaps I shall be broaching during this academic year. Well, I shall do my best ... *or worse*.

2 December 1971

III
I've Been Talking
to Brick Walls

It's not known whether the serial is the principle behind what is serious. Nevertheless, I find myself faced with this question. The question has arisen due to the fact that clearly I cannot continue here what elsewhere is defined as my teaching, as what is called my Seminar, if only because not everyone has been informed that I've been holding a short conversation here once a month. And since there are people who sometimes take the trouble from quite far afield to keep up with what I say elsewhere, under the Seminar title, it wouldn't be right to continue here.

It's a matter of knowing what I'm doing here. It's not altogether what I was expecting. I've been led to change direction by this crowd, a crowd that has ensured that those whom I actually invited to something that was initially called *The Psychoanalyst's Knowledge* are not necessarily absent, but are a little swamped by it. For those who are here, I don't know whether in alluding to my Seminar I'm speaking about something they are familiar with.

They should also take account of the fact that, since last time, I have got this Seminar under way. I've got it under way, and if one is a little attentive and rigorous, one cannot say that this can be done just once. Effectively, it's done twice. And this is why I can say that I've got it under way, because were it not for the second time, there wouldn't be a first.

This holds interest when it comes to calling to mind something I introduced a while ago regarding what is called *repetition*.

Obviously, repetition can only begin with the second time, which turns out to be the one that inaugurates the repetition. If it weren't for the second, there would be no first time. This is the story of 0 and 1. Only, with 1, there cannot be any repetition, such that, for there to be repetition – I don't mean for it to be got under way – there has to be a third.

This seems to have been noticed in relation to God. He only begins with 3. It took people a while to notice, or else they had always known as much but it wasn't noted because, after all, you can't swear to anything in this sense. However, in the end, my dear friend Kojève insisted a great deal on the question of the Christian Trinity.

Be that as it may, from the standpoint that is of interest to us – and what interests us is analytic – clearly this second time is a world away from what I thought I ought to stress in the term *Nachtrag*, retroaction.

These are items that I will try to come back to during the course of this year's Seminar. It's in this respect that what psychoanalysis contributes is a world away from what a certain philosophical tradition has contributed, a tradition that is certainly not negligible, especially as concerns Plato, who underscored very well the value of the dyad. I mean that on this basis, everything hits the skids. What hits the skids? He must have known, but he didn't say.

Be that as it may, it has nothing to do with the analytic *Nachtrag*, with the second time. As for the third, the importance of which I've just emphasized, it is not only for us, it's for God Himself that it takes on importance.

Some time ago, I warmly encouraged everyone to go to see a very beautiful tapestry that was hanging in the Museum of Decorative Arts. On this tapestry you were able to behold the Father, and the Son, and the Holy Spirit represented as utterly the same figure, the figure of a rather noble bearded personage. The three of them were looking at one another. That makes a far stronger impression than beholding someone faced with his own image. With three, it starts to produce a certain effect.

From our point of view as subjects, what might it be for God Himself that can begin with three? This is an old question that I raised very early on, when I was beginning my teaching. I haven't revisited it since. I'll tell you straightaway the answer – it is only from three onwards that He is able to believe in Himself.

It's rather curious that, as far as I know, the following question was never posed – does God believe in Himself? This would, however, be a good example for us. It's altogether striking that this question, which I raised fairly early on, and which I don't believe to be a hollow one, did not apparently give rise to any tumult, at least among my co-religionists, I mean those who were educated in the shadow of the Trinity. I can understand that the rest didn't find it that striking, but these fellows truly are *incoreligionable*. You can't do anything about it.

Yet I did have a few noteworthy people from what is known as the Christian hierarchy. The question arises as to whether they understand nothing because they're right in it, which I find hard to believe, or whether they possess an atheism that is sufficiently complete for this question not to have any effect on them, which is far more likely. I side with this second solution.

It cannot be said that this is what earlier I called a guarantee of seriousness because this atheism might be nothing more than a somnolence, which is fairly commonplace. In other words they don't have the faintest idea of the dimension of the environment in which one may swim. They float on the surface, which is not quite the same thing, and they do so given the fact that they hold one another by the hand. This ends up forming what is known as a network. There is a poem by Paul Fort along those lines – *If all the lasses in the world were to join hands* – this is how it starts – *they could make a ring around the world.* It's a barmy idea because in reality the lasses of the world have never dreamed of doing that. On the other hand, the lads of the world, whom the poem also speaks about, understand one another on that score. They all join hands, and all the more so given that if they didn't, then each lad would have to confront the lass all on his own, and the lads don't care for that. They have to join hands.

It's a different matter for the lasses, though they do get embroiled in it within the context of certain social rites. Take a look at *Danses et légendes de la Chine ancienne*, it's chic. It's even *Shu King* – not shocking. This book was written by a certain Granet, who possessed a kind of genius that has absolutely nothing to do with either ethnology or sinology, though he was incontestably both an ethnologist and a sinologist. He put forward the notion that in ancient China, lasses and lads used to confront one another in equal number. Why not believe him? In practice, from what we know in our times, the lads always group together in a certain number, over a dozen, for the reason I set before you just now – because for each Jack to be all on his own with his Jill carries too many risks.

It's something else for the lasses. Since we're no longer in the time of the *Shu King*, they group together in twos. They're all buddy-buddy with another lass until they snatch a lad away from his regiment. That's right, mister! Whatever you might think, and however shallow these remarks might seem to you, they are grounded on my experience as an analyst. Once she has turned a lad away from his regiment, naturally she drops her best friend, who moreover will tend to fare not so badly in spite of it all.

I'm allowing myself to get a bit carried away. Where do I think I am? One thing led to another and it came out like that, in view of Granet and the astonishing story of what alternates in the poems of the *Shu King*, where there is a choir of lads opposite a choir of lasses. I've let myself get carried away like this, giving a brief newsflash on my analytic experience. This is not the crux of the matter. I won't be setting out the crux of the matter here. But where am I, for me to believe I'm able to speak about the crux of things? I might almost believe I am among *êtres humains*, or even *cousehumains*.[1] This is none the less how I address them.

In the end, it was speaking about my Seminar that led me to get carried away. Since you are perhaps the same people, I spoke as though I were speaking to them, which led me to speak as though I were speaking *about you*, and – who knows? – this has led me to speak as though I were speaking *to you*.

This was not remotely my intention because I came to Sainte-Anne to speak to psychiatrists, and quite clearly not all of you are psychiatrists. Anyhow, what is certain is that this is a bungled action. It's a bungled action that, therefore, runs the risk of being successful at any moment, that is, it could well be the case that I am indeed speaking to someone. How is one to know to whom I am speaking? Especially when, at the end of the day, you count for something in this business, however hard I try. You count at least inasmuch as I'm not speaking where I was counting on speaking, because I was counting on speaking in the Magnan lecture theatre and instead I'm speaking in the chapel.

What a to-do! Did you hear that? *Je parle à la chapelle*. This is the response. I'm speaking to the chapel, that is, to the brick walls. This bungled action is becoming increasingly successful. Now I know to whom I've come to talk, to the very same I've always talked to at Sainte-Anne – to brick walls. It's been an age. Every now and then, I came back with a short lecture title on what I've been teaching, for example. And then a few others, which I'm not going to list. I've always been talking to brick walls here.

Who is it who's got something to say?

Woman in the audience – We should all leave if you're talking to the brick walls.

Who's speaking to me?

Now's the time for me to give a commentary on the fact that talking to brick walls does indeed concern a few people. This is why I asked who spoke up. It's quite certain that, in what used to be called, in times when people were honest, an asylum, a *clinical asylum* as they used to say, the brick walls were no small matter.

I would further say that this chapel strikes me as a site that is extremely well designed when it comes to allowing us to get in touch with what is at issue when I speak of walls. This sort of concession of secularism to the internees, a chapel with its accompaniment of chaplains, well, it's not that it's especially wonderful from the architectural point of view, but in the end it's a chapel with the provision that you would expect of one. It is too frequently omitted that, regardless of the effort architects make to leave them behind, the said architects exist for that, for building walls. And walls, my word — it's altogether striking how, since then, the Christianity I was speaking about earlier has been tending a bit much towards Hegelianism — are made to envelop a void.

How are we to imagine what used to go on within the walls of the Parthenon, and a few other knick-knacks of which some of the crumbled walls still remain? It's very hard to know. What is certain is that we have absolutely no first-hand accounts. We have the sense that, throughout this entire period to which we tack the modern label *paganism*, there were things that went on during various festivals, the names of which have been preserved because there are annals that list the dates of such things — *It was at the Great Panathenaea that Adeimantus and Glaucon*, and so on, you know the rest, *ran into a certain Cephalus*.[2] What used to go on in those festivals? It's quite unbelievable that we don't have the faintest idea.

On the other hand, when it comes to the void, we have a very firm idea about this because everything that remains of what has come down to us from a tradition that is termed *philosophical* accords a major place to the void. There is even a certain Plato who made his entire idea of the world revolve around that. *Idea of the world* really is the right term, because he's the one who invented the cave. He transformed it into a darkroom. There was something going on outside, and, passing through a small aperture, shadows were formed by all that. It may well be here that we have a little thread, a tiny tip of a trace. This is clearly a theory that lets us put a finger on what is involved with the object *a*. Suppose if you will that Plato's cave is equivalent to these walls within which my voice is making itself heard. It's quite clear that I derive jouissance from these walls. And it is in this respect that you all obtain jouissance, every one of you, through participation. Seeing me talking to brick walls is something that cannot leave you indifferent. And reflect on this – just imagine that Plato had been a structuralist, then he would have realized what is truly involved in the cave, namely that this is undoubtedly where language was born.

This has to be turned around. For a long time now mankind has been mewling, like any other little animal, whining for mother's milk. However, he's known for a good while that he's capable of doing something with this babbling and gibbering in which everything is produced. In order to choose, he must have realized that a *k* will better resound at the far end of the cave, and that a *b* or a *p* will come out better at the entrance. This is where he heard their resonance.

I've been letting myself get carried away this evening because I've been talking to brick walls.

You shouldn't think I'm saying I didn't get anything else out of Sainte-Anne.

I only got round to talking at Sainte-Anne very late in the day. I mean that the idea didn't occur to me, apart from carrying out a few minor duties when I was clinical director. I used to recount a few brief stories to the student interns, and this was even where I learnt to watch my step about the stories I recount. One day I was telling the story of a patient's mother, the mother of a charming homosexual man whom I was analysing. Unable to avoid seeing this one coming – the twisted woman in question – she came out with the exclamation, *And there was me thinking he was impotent!*[3] I told the story and ten people in the audience – there weren't only students – recognized her immediately. It could only be her. You have a sudden realization of what it means to be a person of society! Naturally, this became a big deal, because I was reproached for it, even though I had repeated absolutely not a word more than this tremendous exclamation. This has inspired me since to be far more prudent when discussing cases. But, anyway, this is yet another little digression. Let's pick up the thread.

Before I started talking here, I did a good many

other things at Sainte-Anne, if only by way of turning up each day and fulfilling my responsibilities. As far as my discourse is concerned, everything starts off from this. If I've been talking to brick walls, it's because I got down to it rather late. Long before I heard what these walls were sending back to me, that is, my own voice preaching in the desert – this is a reply to the person who spoke about leaving – I heard things that were utterly decisive, for me in any case. But this is my own business. I mean that those whose status confines them to these walls are quite capable of making themselves heard, provided the appropriate lugs are within earshot.

To spell it right out, and to pay homage to something in which, all told, she had no personal involvement, it was, as is widely known, in connection with the patient to whom I tacked the name Aimée, which of course wasn't her real name, that I was drawn in towards psychoanalysis.

There wasn't only her, of course. There were others before her, and then there were a fair few to whom I gave the floor. This is what my patient presentations consist in, which is a kind of exercise that consists in listening to patients.

Obviously this is not something that happens to them on every street corner. It so happens that in speaking afterwards with a few people who are there to accompany me and to grasp from it what they can, I learn something from it. Afterwards, not straightaway. Clearly one has to tune one's voice to the reverberation off the walls.

What I am going to try to call into question at my Seminar this year will revolve around the relationship between psychoanalysis and logic, which is something to which I accord great importance.

I learnt very early on that logic is capable of incurring the world's odium. That was at a time when I used to read a certain Abelard, attracted by goodness knows what odour of a fly.[4] For my part, I can't say that logic made me absolutely odious to anyone, save a few psychoanalysts. Perhaps it's because I manage seriously to buffer its meaning.

I manage this with much greater ease because I absolutely do not believe in common sense. There is *sens*, meaning, but there is no common variety. In all likelihood, not a single one of you hears me in the same sense as another. Furthermore, I endeavour to make it so that access to this meaning is not so easy, which entails you having to put something of your own into it, which is a salubrious secretion, and even a therapeutic one. Secrete meaning with vigour and you will see how much easier life becomes.

It was precisely through this that I came to notice the existence of the object *a*, the seedling of which each of you possesses, waiting to sprout. What constitutes its force, and by the same stroke the force of every one of you in particular, is that the object *a* is utterly foreign to the question of meaning. Meaning is a little paint roughly daubed on this object *a*, to which each of you has your own particular attachment.

It has nothing to do with either meaning or reason. The question on the agenda is that many tend to reduce reason to *reson*. Spell it *r. e. s. o. n.* Indulge me. This is how Francis Ponge puts it.[5] Being a poet, and being the great poet he is, we ought to make sure we don't fail to take into account what he tells us on this question. He's not the only one. It's a very grave question that I've only seen formulated seriously, besides this poet, by mathematicians, namely the question as to what reason, which for the time being we shall be content to grasp as emanating from

87

the grammatical apparatus, has to do with something that – I don't want to say something that would be intuitive, because that would amount to falling back onto the slope of intuition, that is, something visual – but precisely with something that is resonant.

Is that which resonates the origin of the *res*, from which reality is wrought? This is a question that touches on everything that may be extracted from language in the capacity of logic. It is widely known that logic is not sufficient, and that for some time now it has needed – this could have been seen making an appearance some time ago, precisely with Plato – to bring mathematics into play. It is here that the question arises as to where this real is to be centred, the real to which logical examination leads us, and which turns out to lie at the mathematical level.

There are mathematicians who tell that on no account can one base oneself on this so-called formalist junction, this mathematico-logical junction, that there is something beyond, something to which all these intuitive references serve to pay homage, and which people thought they would be able to purge from this mathematics. They search, in this beyond, to find out which *reson* they should turn to in order to reach what is at issue, namely the real.

Of course, I won't be able to broach it this evening. What I can say is that it was from one particular angle, that of a logic, that I was able – on a path that, starting off from my patient Aimée, culminated, in the Seminar of the year before last, in setting out the four discourses, to which converges the scrutiny of certain items of contemporary pertinence – to do what? Well, at least to spell out the reason for the walls.

Indeed, for anyone who dwells here within these walls, the walls of the clinical asylum, it would be as well to know that what situates and defines the psychiatrist as such is his situation in relation to these walls, these walls whereby secularism has created, on the inside, an exclusion of madness and of what madness means. This can only be broached along the path of an analysis of discourse.

Truth be told, so little analysis was practised before me that it's accurate to say that there was never on the part of the psychoanalysts the slightest disagreement with the psychiatrist's position. Yet one can find collected in my *Écrits* something that I was making heard way back, before 1950, under the title *Propos sur la causalité psychique.* In this talk I took a stand against any definition of mental illness that took shelter behind the construction built from a semblance which, though going by the label *organo-dynamism*, swept none the less to one side what is at issue in the segregation of mental illness, namely something that is other, that is yoked to a certain discourse, the one I've been pinpointing as the discourse of the master.

Again, history has shown that this discourse was alive and kicking for centuries in a way that was profitable for everyone up until a particular inflection, whereupon, by virtue of a fractional slippage that went unnoticed by the very people concerned by it, it turned into the discourse of the capitalist, of which we wouldn't have had the faintest idea had Marx not set himself to completing it, to giving it its subject, the proletariat. Thanks to this, the discourse of capitalism has flourished in every nation-state that has taken a Marxist form.

What differentiates the discourse of capitalism is *Verwerfung*, the fact of rejecting, outside all the fields of the symbolic. This brings with it the consequence I have already said it has. What does it reject? Well, castration. Any order, any discourse that aligns itself with capitalism, sweeps to one side what we may simply call, my fine friends, matters of love. You see, it's a mere nothing.

This was precisely why, two centuries after this slippage, which after all we may call a Calvinist slippage, castration finally made its irruptive entrance in the form of the analytic discourse. Naturally, the analytic discourse still hasn't bloody got round to providing so much as a slither of an articulation of this, but ultimately it did propagate the metaphor of it and realize that all metonymies stemmed from it.

There you have it. It was in the name of this, carried along by a sort of hubbub that emerged somewhere on the side of the psychoanalysts, that I was led to introduce the evident factor in what was novel about psychoanalysis, namely that it was a matter of language and that it was a new discourse.

As I have told you, the object *a* in person is the position – one cannot say that the psychoanalyst brings himself to it – to which the psychoanalyst is brought by his analysand. The question I ask is, *how is it that an analysand could ever yearn to become a psychoanalyst?* It's imponderable. They come to it like the marbles in some backgammon sets, which you are well acquainted with. They end up dropping into the side tray. They come along without the faintest idea of what's happening to them. Well, once they are there, they're in it, and at that point something awakens. This is why I proposed to study it.

Be that as it may, at the time this hustle and bustle among the marbles was produced, there are no words to describe the jocundity in which I wrote *Function and Field of Speech and Language*. How was it that, out of all sorts of other sensible things, I picked an epigraph of the ritornello kind, which you can find in the third section? It was a thing I found in an almanac called *Paris en l'an 2000*. It was not lacking in talent, although since then no one has heard the name of the fellow whose name I cite – I'm a decent chap – and who relates this thing that pops up awkwardly in this *Function and Field* affair. It begins like this:

> Entre l'homme et la femme,
> > Il y a l'amour.
> Entre l'homme et l'amour,
> > Il y a un monde.

Entre l'homme et le monde,
    Il y a un mur.[6]

You see, I foresaw what I would be telling you this evening – I've been talking to brick walls. You're going to see that this has nothing to do with the next chapter, but I couldn't resist. Since I've been talking to brick walls here, I'm not teaching a course, so I'm not going to tell you what in Jakobson's terms is enough to justify these six lines of doggerel being poetry none the less, proverbial poetry. It drones along. *Entre l'homme et la femme / Il y a l'amour.* Why, of course! There is but that. And, *Entre l'homme et l'amour / Il y a un monde.* When one says *there is a world*, it means, *as for you, you'll never get there.* Even so, at the start it says, *Entre l'homme et la femme / Il y a l'amour.* Between man and woman, there is love. This means that it bonds. A world, meanwhile, floats. Yet when it comes to *Il y a un mur*, you will have understood that *entre* means interposition, because it's very ambiguous, this *entre*. Elsewhere, at my Seminar, we will be speaking about mesology. What holds the function of *entre*? But here we are in poetic ambiguity and, it has to be said, it's well worth it.

93

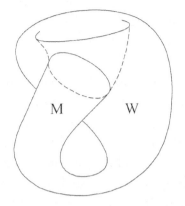

What I have just drawn on this swivelling blackboard is one way, as good a way as any other, of representing the Klein bottle. It's a surface that has particular topological properties. Those of you who are not familiar with it will have to look it up. It looks a lot like a Möbius band, that is, something you can make simply by twisting a little strip of paper and gluing the ends together after a half-twist. Only, in this case it's a tube. It's a tube that at a certain point turns back upon itself. I don't want to say that this is its topological definition. It's a way of illustrating it, which I have already used often enough for some of the people here to know what I'm speaking about.

The hypothesis is that, between man and

woman, there should be a ring, right here, as Paul Fort was saying earlier. So, I've put man on the left and woman on the right. This is pure convention. I could have put them the other way round. Let's try to see topologically what it was that pleased me in these six short lines of verse by Antoine Tudal, to cite him by name.

Between man and woman, there is love. This is communication at full throttle. You can see that it circulates. It pools together the flux, the influx and everything that gets added to it when one is an obsessional, for instance, oblativity, the obsessional's sensational invention. Love is here, this little ring, which is everywhere, except that there is a place at which it will turn back, and in one hell of a way. But let's stay in the first phase. Between man, on the left, and woman, on the right, there is love. It's the little ring. I just told you that this character goes by the name of Antoine. Don't ever imagine that any of my words are surplus to requirement. This was to tell you that he belongs to the male sex, which means that he sees things from his side.

It's a matter now of seeing what will come next. How can it be written? What will there be between man, that is, him the pouet – the pouet of *Pouasie* as dear Léon-Paul Fargue once said – and love?[7] Am I going to have to go back to the blackboard? You saw just now that this was a somewhat unsteady exercise. Well, not at all, because even so, on the left, he occupies the entire space. Therefore, what there is between him and love is precisely what's on the other side, that is, in the right-hand portion of the diagram. *Between man and love, there is a world*, which means that this covers the territory initially occupied by woman, where I have written *W*, in the right-hand portion. It is for this reason that the one whom we shall call man on this occasion imagines to himself that he *knows*, in the biblical sense, the world. This knowing is quite simply the sort of dream of knowledge that comes to the place of what has been labelled with the *W* of woman in the diagram.

This enables us to see what is at issue topologically when we are told, next, *Between man and the world* – this world that is substituted for the volatilization of the sexual partner – *there is a wall*. The wall is the site at which the turning back occurs, which the other day I introduced as the signifier of the junction between truth and knowledge. I'm not the one who said there was a

96

cut. It was a poet from *Papouasie* who said there was a wall. It's not a wall. It's simply the locus of castration. This means that knowledge leaves the field of truth intact, and vice versa.

Yet what you have to see is that this wall is everywhere, because it is what defines the surface. The circle, or the turning point – let's say the circle because I've represented it here as a circle – is homogeneous across the entire surface. This means that you would be wrong to represent it in your minds as a surface that can be represented intuitively. If I were to show you right now the sort of cut that would be sufficient instantaneously to render this surface volatile, in terms of something that would be specific and topologically defined, you would see that it's not a surface one can represent to oneself, but rather something that is defined by particular coordinates – call them vector coordinates if you like – such that the turn is always there in each of the points across the surface. As for the relation between man and woman, and everything that results from it with regard to either partner, namely his or her position as well as his or her knowledge, this means that castration is everywhere.

Love, the love that this conveys, that flows, that gushes, this is what love is, isn't it? Love, the good that a mother wishes her son, *l'(a)mur*, you just have to put brackets around the *a* to meet once more what we experience first hand on a daily basis, namely that even between mother and son, the mother's relation to castration counts a fair bit.

To get a sound idea of what love is, one should perhaps base oneself on the fact that when it is played out seriously between a man and a woman, it always entails the stake of castration. It is what castrates. What is it that files down this narrow pass of castration? This is something we shall be trying to broach along paths that ought to be somewhat rigorous. They can only be rigorous by being logical, and even topological.

I've been speaking with the *murs* here, indeed with *(a)murs*, and with a-*murs*-ement. Elsewhere, at my Seminar, I am trying to account for this. And whatever use the walls might have when it comes to keeping the voice in shape, it's clear that the walls cannot, any more than the rest, have any intuitive support, even with all the architect's art into the bargain.

The four discourses that I mentioned earlier are essential when it comes to ascertaining what it is that you are the subjects of, always, regardless of what you are doing. And you are always subjects who are *supposed* relative to what occurs by dint of a signifier that is clearly the master of the game. In regard to something that is other, not to say the Other, you are merely what is *supposed* by it. You don't give it any meaning. You don't have enough of it yourselves for that. But you do flesh out this signifier that represents you, the master signifier.

Well, what you are in all of this, shadowy shades that you are, don't imagine that the substance that is attributed to you in this eternal dreaming is anything other than the jouissance from which you are cut off. How can one fail to see what is akin here to the substantial invocation and the unbelievable myth of sexual jouissance, which Freud himself deigned to echo? This sexual jouissance is an object that goes speeding along, like in the hunt-the-ring parlour game, but the status of which no one is capable of stating, if not to say that it is precisely the *supreme* status. It is the *supreme* of a curve, to which it gives its meaning, and also, very precisely, the supreme of which escapes. Moreover, psychoanalysis takes its decisive step in being able to articulate the array of different types of sexual jouissance. What psychoanalysis demonstrates is precisely that the jouissance that might be called *sexual*, in inverted commas, the jouissance that would not be a semblance of the sexual, bears the stamp of nothing more, until further notice, than what is not stated, than what is not announced, except as the index of castration.

I reconstruct the walls as they are logically, prior to assuming a status and a form. The barred S, the S_1, the S_2, and the *a* that I toyed around with for you for a few months, all of this is nevertheless the last wall behind which you can place the meaning of what concerns us. We believe we know what this means – truth and semblance, jouissance and surplus jouissance. But even so, in relation to what equally has no need of walls in order to be written, these terms, which are like the four cardinal points in relation to which you have to situate what you are, a psychiatrist could notice perfectly well that he is bound to the walls by a definition of discourse. For what do psychiatrists have to deal with? Well, with no other malady but the one that is defined by the Act of

30 June 1838, namely *someone who is dangerous to himself and to others*.

This is very curious, this introduction of danger into the discourse through which social order is established. What is this danger? *Dangerous to themselves*, well, this is the very lifeblood of society, and *dangerous to others*, Lord knows that every liberty is left to each individual in this sense.

In our age, I've been seeing protests against the use that is made – to call a spade a spade and to hurry up a bit, because it's getting late – of asylums in the USSR, or of something that has to go by a more pretentious name, so as to shield away objectors, let's say. It's quite obvious that they are dangerous for the social order into which they are integrated.

What is it that separates, what distance is there, between the way of opening the doors of psychiatric hospitals in a place where the capitalist discourse is perfectly coherent with itself, and a place like ours, where it is still in its infancy? The first thing that psychiatrists, if there are a few of them here, could get – I won't say from my speech, which has nothing to do with this business – but from the reflection of my voice off these brick walls, is to know first and foremost what it is that specifies them as psychiatrists.

This does not stop them, within the limits of these walls, from hearing something other than my voice. The voice, for example, of those who are interned here, because, after all, it can lead somewhere, to the point of forming an accurate idea of what is involved in the object *a*.

I have shared a few reflections with you this evening, and of course these are reflections to which my person as such is no stranger. This is what I most loathe in others, because after all, among the people who hearken to me once in a while, and who for that are called, Lord knows why, my pupils, it cannot be said that they dispense with reflecting. The *mur* can always function as a *muroir*.

It is doubtless because of this that I have come back here to spill some stuff at Sainte-Anne. It was not, strictly speaking, out of delusion, but even so, something of these walls was still weighing on my heart.

If I can, with time, manage to succeed in building the *reson d'être*, however you write it, with my barred S, my S_1, my S_2, and the object *a*, perhaps after all you will not take the reflection of my voice off these walls for a mere personal reflection.

6 January 1972

Appendix

In the fourth talk (3 February 1972), Lacan announces that he intends to clarify remarks he had made during the Seminar ... or Worse, *but the opening picks up where the third talk left off. The relevant extract is reproduced hereunder.* – JAM.

Last time I told you I had been *talking to brick walls.* I gave a commentary on this remark, which was articulated in harmony with what surrounds us. A particular little diagram, the one that draws on the Klein bottle, was used to reassure those who might have felt excluded by the wording. As I explained at length, what is addressed to the walls has the property of reverberating. That I should have been speaking in that way, indirectly, was certainly not designed to offend anyone, because, after all, it can't be said that this is a special privilege of my discourse.

Regarding this wall, which is on no account a metaphor, I would like today to clarify what I have been saying elsewhere, at my Seminar. Since it's not a matter of just any knowledge, but rather the psychoanalyst's knowledge, this will justify my not doing it at my Seminar.

To give something of an introduction, to suggest a dimension to some of you, I will say that one cannot *talk of love*, as they say, except in an imbecilic or abject manner. *Abject* is a change for the worse. That's how people speak about it in psychoanalysis. However, that one may write about love is something that ought to be quite striking.

It's clear that the letter, the *lettre d'amur* – to pick up from the little six-line ballad I commented on here last time – will have to chase its own tail. It begins *Entre l'homme* – no one knows what that is – *et l'amour, il y a la femme.* Between man and love, there is woman. Then it continues until it comes to an end with the *mur*. Between man and the wall, there is, precisely, *amur*, the love letter. The best thing in this curious impulse called love, which gets flattened somewhere, is the letter.

The letter can assume rather odd shapes. There was one fellow, some three thousand years ago, who was certainly at the height of his success, his success in love, who saw something appearing on the wall. I have already commented on this so I'm not about to go over it. It said, *MENE, MENE, TEKEL, UPHARSIN*, which, I don't know why, is voiced *MENE, TEKEL, PERES*.[1] As I have explicated a few times, letters arrive always at the destination. Luckily they arrive too late, besides how uncommon they are. It can also happen that they arrive on time. These are the rare cases when appointments are not missed. There are not many cases in history when *things arrive*, as happened to this nondescript Nebuchadnezzar.

As an opener, I'm not going to push this any further, even if it means taking it up later, because in the way I have presented it to you, this *amur* has nothing especially amusing about it. Yet for my part I can support myself only by amusing, whether it be a serious or comical amusement. What I explained last time was that the serious amusement would be going on elsewhere, in a place where I'm being accommodated, and that I was reserving the comical amusements for here. I don't know whether I shall be altogether up to it this evening, perhaps due to this opening on the *lettre d'amur*. Nevertheless, I will try.

[...]

Translator's Notes

I Knowledge, Ignorance, Truth and Jouissance

1 Lacan introduced the neologism *poubellication* – a condensation of *poubelle* and *publication* – in *Seminar XIII* (lesson of 15 December 1965) and often used the term thereafter to denote his own published writings. Cf. 'D'un dessein', in *Écrits* (Paris: Seuil, 1966, p. 364).

2 Paul Morand described the crowded metropolitan experience of modern France as *le camp de concentration du Bon Dieu* (*France la doulce*, Paris: 1934, p. 218). The phrase was widely used prior to the Second World War and the discovery of the Nazi concentration camps.

3 The 1967 *Vocabulaire de la psychanalyse* by Laplanche and Pontalis was translated into English as *The Language of Psychoanalysis* (New York: Norton, 1973).

4 August Weismann used the Latinate *soma*, but not *germen*, which was chiefly an intervention of French translators and commentators to refer to *Keimplasma*, 'germ-plasm' (occasionally 'germinative plasma' in English), the substance of *Keimzellen*, 'germ cells'. In the sixth section of *Jenseits des Lustprinzips*, Freud alternates between *Keimplasma* and *Keimzellen*.

5 Assuming the transcription to be dependable (as a rule, Lacan provides a commentary on his neologisms when introducing them, but this is not the case here), the coinage *éffloupi* includes the adjective *flou* ('hazy' or 'woolly') with possible overtones of 'effluence/effluent' or 'ephemeral'.

6 Literally, 'chase away the natural and it will come back at a gallop', the French alexandrine, adapted by Destouches in his 1732 play *Le Glorieux* (III, 5) from Horace's first book of Epistles (10, 24: *naturam expelles furca, tamen*

usque recurret), indicates that one cannot conceal one's 'true nature' indefinitely. Common English-language equivalents to the French proverbial use are 'what's bred in the bone comes out in the flesh', and 'a leopard can't change its spots'.

II On Incomprehension and Other Themes

1 The French *entretien* is derived from the verb *entretenir*, 'to maintain' or 'to keep up', which is commonly used in the reflexive form to denote conversation or discussion. Depending on context, the noun translates as 'interview', 'consultation', or 'a (formal) talk'.

2 Here, Lacan is driving a fine distinction between *significatif* and *signifiant*, which is not easily conveyed in English. The former adjective lies more on the side of the 'meaningful', whereas the latter, in its equivalence to the noun form ('signifier'), highlights 'signifierness' at one remove from its capture in the linguistic sign that allows for the production of meaning. *Faire signe* also carries the more colloquial sense of beckoning or 'letting know', especially through non-verbal gestures such as a wave of the hand or a nod of the head.

3 Though *chiffre* would more conventionally be rendered as 'number' or '(numerical) figure', we have opted for its English cognate 'cipher' to accommodate the operation of enciphering a value into a number or a letter.

4 The pronunciation of the French *allée* is identical to *aller*. An *aller-simple* is a single outbound journey, and *aller-retour* a return.

5 This is the earliest recorded occurrence of Lacan's recycling of the Greek μάθημα, 'that which is learnt'.

114

The term is reminiscent of the *mythème* that Claude Lévi-Strauss introduced in *The Structural Study of Myth* (1955), there defined as a 'gross constituent unit' of mythological constructions, and which itself came in echo of the linguistic 'phoneme' (first conceptualized by Jan Baudouin de Courtenay). It should be noted that whereas recent commentators have retrojected 'matheme' to cover Lacan's earlier algebraic notations and diagrammatic schemata, Lacan himself restricts the term to articulated 'algorithmic' structures in which 'the mathematizable is formulated in impasses' ('L'étourdit', July 1972). Thus, each of the four 'tetrahedral' discourses is a matheme, while, according to Lacan's remark at the 1976 EFP Study Days, the discrete notation S(Ⱥ) is not (*Lettres de l'École freudienne de Paris*, issue 21, 1977, p. 507).

6 The phrasing of *à partir de l'être parlant* could be understood either as 'on the basis of (the) speaking being' or 'on the basis of (their) being speaking'.

7 There is a pun here on the near homophony between *l'émoi* and *le mois*, alluding to the civil unrest in France in the month of May 1968. *Faire l'émoi* is 'to cause turmoil' or 'to make a commotion'. See also Lacan's etymological enquiry, drawing on the Block and von Wartburg entries for *émeute* and *émouvoir*, in *Book X* of the Seminar (Cambridge: Polity, 2014, pp. 12–13).

8 The latter spelling, *l'Achose*, features in the written text 'Lituraterre', penned in May 1971 and first published in the third issue of the magazine *Littérature* in October 1971. The English-language translation of this text offers 'th'Athing' (*Hurly-Burly*, 2013, 9: 34). The prefixed 'A' functions as both a privative and as

object *a*. See also Lacan's comment below on '*achosique* being'.

III   I've Been Talking to Brick Walls

1   *Cousehumains* is loosely homophonic with *cousu(s) main*: literally 'hand-stitched', and, in some contexts, 'top-notch'.

2   What is known is divided, of course, between the written and the remembered: in the *Parmenides* (126–7), Adeimantus and Glaucon come across Cephalus of Clazomenae in the Athenian Agora, whereupon the latter mentions the story that begins with the arrival, some years previously, of Zeno of Elea and Parmenides at the Great Panathenaea.

3   The way Lacan relates the story here, it is not altogether clear who was speaking to whom. On page 104 of the *Écrits*, we can read that the patient's mother snapped directly at her son, 'And I thought you were impotent!' in response to him confiding in her his homosexual leanings.

4   Lacan says *odeur de mouche*, punning on a phrase from the opening of Abelard's 'Confessio fidei ad Heloissam': *odiusum me mundo reddidit logica*.

5   Serge Gavronsky, in 'Ardens Organum, selections from *Pour un Malherbe*', drops the accent from *réson* in his Englished renderings (Ponge, F., *The Power of Language: Texts and Translations*, University of California, 1979, pp. 230–1, 248–9, 252–3). We have followed suit here.

6   Lacan does not reproduce the opening three lines as they appear in the first epigraph to section III of *Fonction et champ de la parole et du langage* (*Écrits*, p. 289). There, as

in the 1945 collection *SouSpente* in which the poem first featured under the title 'Obstacles', and in its 1949 reprint in *Almanach de 1950, Paris en l'an 2000*, the first stanza opens: 'Entre l'homme et l'amour / Il y a la femme. / Entre l'homme et la femme [...]'. The full poem may be rendered as follows:

> Between man and love,
>> There is woman.
> Between man and woman,
>> There is a world.
> Between man and the world,
>> There is a wall.

In a letter dated March 1954, the painter Nicolas de Staël notes that his stepson Antoine Tudal (who previously went by the name Antek Teslar) was just twelve years old when he composed the poem.

7   From 'Air du poète' (1923):

> Au pays de Papouasie
> J'ai caressé la Pouasie ...
> La grâce que je vous souhaite
> C'est de n'être pas Papouète.

Peter Low has rendered the poem as follows:

> **Song of the Poet**
> On the shores of Papoetan Bayee
> I stroked the skin of Poetrayee
> For you I wish the blest condition
> Of not being Papetician.

And Christopher Goldsack, thus:

Poet's Air
In the country of Papua
I caressed the Papuane ...
The fortune that I wish you
Is not to be Papuan.

Appendix

1 Daniel (5:25–9) is interpreting the written nouns as verbs.